# Little Songs of the Geisha

# Little Songs of the Geisha

## Traditional Japanese Ko-Uta

Liza Dalby

TUTTLE PUBLISHING
Boston · Rutland, Vermont · Tokyo

First published in 1979 as *Ko-Uta* by Tuttle Publishing, an imprint of
Periplus Editions (HK) Ltd, with editorial offices at 153 Milk Street,
Boston, Massachusetts 02109.

Library of Congress Catalog Card Number: 78-66085
ISBN: 0-8048-3250-1

Distributed by

**North America**
Tuttle Publishing
Distribution Center
Airport Industrial Park
364 Innovation Drive
North Clarendon, VT
05759-9436
Tel: (802) 773-8930
Tel: (800) 526-2778
Fax: (802) 773-6993

**Japan**
Tuttle Publishing
RK Building, 2nd Floor
2-13-10 Shimo-Meguro,
Meguro-Ku
Tokyo 153 0064
Tel: (03) 5437-0171
Fax: (03) 5437-0755

**Asia Pacific**
Berkeley Books Pte Ltd
5 Little Road #08-01
Singapore 536983
Tel: (65) 280-1330
Fax: (65) 280-6290

1  3  5  7  9  10  8  6  4  2
06  05  04  03  02  01  00

Cover design by Laura Shaw
Cover photograph © Michael Maslan Historic Photographs/Corbis
Printed in the United States of America

*To Hasui Kiyo*

## TABLE OF CONTENTS

Appendixes:

へ小唄〉

# INTRODUCTION

As a genre of music, the *ko-uta* is best described by a direct translation of the word—literally, "little song." Most *ko-uta* may be sung in less than a minute, longer ones taking perhaps three or four at most. They are accompanied by the *shamisen*—a fretless, three-stringed, long-necked, "banjo-like" instrument. The difficulty in singing *ko-uta* lies in the fact that voice and instrument take two separate threads of sound and interval, weaving them together like a duet. The shamisen gives the initial note of a phrase, leading the singer, and after that it is the complicated timing and skillful juxtaposition of shamisen and voice which is appreciated.

It is difficult to convey the musical aspect on the written page, but the aim of this sampling from the *ko-uta* repertoire is to introduce in a small way the fascinating diversity of these songs. Ranging from the most refined aestheticism to earthy humor, *ko-uta* have been created from many sources. Like *haiku*, they are an extremely

9

short medium of expression; thus, their essence is pithiness. They must make their point in few words, so they tend to be "dense" in the sense that many images may be evoked with a few well-chosen phrases.

*Ko-uta* come to life when they are sung, and the best example of where they live is in the geisha world. Most geisha study and perform *ko-uta,* and many of the songs concern male-female relations in the pleasure quarters.

Unlike *haiku* and the other forms of Japanese poetry thus far introduced to the West that come from the aristocratic world or from the "wandering monk" tradition, *ko-uta* belong to the hardworking, hard-playing merchant class of the late Edo period (mainly 19th century). The rise of the geisha coincided with the rise in prosperity of this class, and *ko-uta* express the sentiments of sophisticated Edo (now Tokyo) city dwellers at play.

One concept essential to an understanding of *ko-uta* is that of *iroke.* One of those frustratingly untranslatable terms, *iroke* is written with two characters, 色気, one meaning "color" (*iro*), the other "feeling" (*ke* or *ki*). *Iro* in this case most closely approximates the meaning of "eroticism"—but in a milder sense than the English word conveys. *Ke* means something along the lines of "character" or "spirit."

As there is no precise English equivalent, the best way to proceed is to give examples of the semantic context in which *iroke* appears. Many of the *ko-uta* themselves are prime illustrations of *iroke,* but a few preliminary words may help the reader approach them with a deeper understanding.

*Iroke* is sensuality; it is evoked by images which appeal to the senses. It denotes attraction felt between the sexes in the passing of a glance or the swish of a trailing kimono. The essence of *iroke* is understatement. The minute it becomes obvious it ceases to be *iroke*. It is a subtle atmosphere created by the contact of two people. It cannot exist in the abstract, and it is not as blatant as "sex appeal." It implies intimacy in that it becomes lost in an impersonal situation.

Some examples of *iroke* are: the tiny glimpse of red which lines the geisha's formal black kimono, seen against the white of the powdered nape of her neck; the sidelong glance, exchanged without a word, between a man and a woman; playing the shamisen with the fingernail instead of the large ivory plectrum; the four-and-a-half-mat tatami room (*yojōhan*) which is just big enough for two people and a small table; the *kotatsu*, or quilt-covered table under which feet may be talking while faces above show no sign; one strand of hair loose in an otherwise perfect coiffure.

The geisha probably best understand and embody *iroke*. It is a middle state between the elegant, refined, but somewhat unapproachable "proper lady," and the obvious come-on of the rather loud, conventionally "sexy" bar hostess.

The most welcome guests in the geisha world are, conversely, the men who have *iroke*, and more often than not these customers are quite familiar with *ko-uta*. They will have the geisha pick up the *shamisen* and accompany them, and though their voices may falter, the geisha keeps the rhythm by strategically placed "calls" (*kakegoe*) marking the phrases.

It is impossible to describe a form which applies to all *ko-uta* because of the diversity of the songs. The lines basically follow a pattern of seven and five syllables, which has been an almost "natural" rhythm for Japanese poetry since about the 6th century. While there are no strict rules for *ko-uta* as there are for *waka* or *haikai renga,* which are defined by their 5–7–5–7–7 structure, there is a decided preference for the sense of the phrases to follow a seven-five pattern rather than a five-seven one. So even when the verse starts out with a line of five syllables, it usually switches to a pattern in which a seven-syllable phrase is followed by a five-syllable line.

In almost every case, the last line is one of five syllables, whether it is ending a phrase or the whole song, though occasionally different rhythm endings of even-numbered syllables are used for an odd effect. Several songs are in continuous seven-five couplets. In general, the more "serious" or "classical" the piece, the closer it adheres to the seven-and-five syllable pattern. Some of the more frivolous pieces contain unorthodox rhythms to bring out the bantering tone of the song.

〈 小 唄 〉

STRUCTURE

While it is by no means true for all *ko-uta,* we find that

many have a common structure in first sketching a natural scene, followed by a middle or pivot phrase which connects the description of nature to the last section, which talks of some human emotion. This technique is one commonly found in traditional poetry such as *waka* and *haiku*.

The "pivot words," or *kakekotoba*, finish one phrase while at the same time being the start of a new thought, so the phrases are inextricably tied. This kind of poetry can lead the mind from a descriptive scene to a human sentiment without a break. Also, with the large number of homophones in Japanese, the possibilities for double meanings are endless, and endlessly used in *ko-uta*.

*Ko-uta* enjoyed popularity in the worldly-wise city of Edo (Tokyo), where they were composed and enjoyed by an ingroup which prided itself on its sophisticated entertainments. Some of the songs employ obscure or special slang phrases that were familiar only to those in the know. While some of the sentiments are vulgar, the style and expression are anything but. Along with this, there are certain "loaded" words that appear frequently and which have the power to evoke a wide range of emotional nuance for those of the *ko-uta* world.

The musical structure of *ko-uta* in every case follows the text. That is, there are no "tunes" that exist on their own to which text would be added later. Often the musical mode changes to correspond with an emotional shift in the text, as can be clearly seen in the Western notation provided for *Tomete mo Kaeru* (the title represents the first phrase of the Japanese text; this is *ko-uta* number 6 in this selection). Such shifts make it difficult to ascertain the tonal center of a piece. In the last section of *Tomete mo Kaeru* the modes are combined and ultimately resolved by a return to the initial cadence pattern. This tendency can be found in many of the songs.

The tempo and register of any song is left to the discretion of the performer, and some liberties can be taken with ornamentation, particularly of the vocal line.

To help give the reader some idea of how a *ko-uta* sounds, I have included the score for *Tomete mo Kaeru* at the back of the book. The score is provided both in traditional *shamisen* notation and in a transposition into Western notation.


HISTORY

There were short lyric songs going by the name *ko-uta* far back in Japanese history. The first collection of such was compiled in 1518, and called *Kanginshū*. In the early 17th century, Rōsai Ryūtatsu, a prolific composer of these songs, put out a collection of his own work, and there is another famous compilation called *Matsu no Ha* from about a hundred years later.

The prototype of the *shamisen* was imported to Japan around 1600, and it was soon used as an accompaniment to native folk songs. Out of this practice developed the *utaimono*, or "lyric *shamisen* music," and from this style came the ditties collectively called *ko-uta*—now using a different character for *uta* which designates a "song" rather than a "poem."

〈小唄〉

When the *shamisen* was first used as musical accompaniment for the early forms of Kabuki (sometime before 1650), the music was a type of *ko-uta* or *ha-uta* (also meaning "short song"). Gradually these were found to lack the sustaining power to carry the longer dance forms being developed, and a new type of music, *naga-uta* ("long songs"), was composed. By 1740, *naga-uta* was a complete style in itself, and formed the musical backbone for the highly popular Kabuki drama. *Ko-uta* and *ha-uta,* as emotional and sentimental small lyrics, continued to be sung in the geisha districts.

The *ko-uta* of the late 17th century are notable for certain excesses of erotic expression, which finally led governmental authorities to order reform. The style *utazawa,* of the 18th century, was a result of this, and attempted to create a more refined short lyric.

The distinction between *ko-uta* and *ha-uta* is not always easy to draw. In general, *ha-uta* may be thought of as arising from the more stately *ji-uta* tradition of the Kansai region (western Japan, including Kyoto), and *ko-uta* as being lighter, more erotic music from Edo. There has been much mingling of influences though, and both forms, along with the now rarely heard *utazawa* style, recreate a sentimental mood of the Tokugawa period for modern listeners.

By the Meiji period (1868–1912), the musical form *ko-uta* as we hear it now was set. It attained great popularity, overshadowing the similar *ha-uta* and *utazawa* styles. New songs were composed and different stylistic schools arose. Kasuga, the style I studied, is one of these.

Right after the Second World War, perhaps in a burst

of nostalgia for times past, *ko-uta* were so much in fashion that people spoke of a "*ko-uta* boom." The tradition of eclecticism continued, and inspiration came from new sources. One, derived from the Puccini opera *Madame Butterfly*, is called "My Love Is in America," and is a *ko-uta* rendition of Chocho-san's lament for the fickle Pinkerton.

*     *     *

I first discovered *ko-uta* while conducting a socio-anthropological study of the geisha as a traditional subculture within modern Japanese society. Part of the study involved "becoming a geisha" for a year and part of this meant learning to sing *ko-uta* while accompanying myself on the *shamisen*. It must be said that a year is entirely too short a time to master the *shamisen*, but I had the advantage of nine years of study of *naga-uta* ("long songs"), which contain bits of *ko-uta* style. I began translating the various songs as I came to master them, and this selection of 25 songs evolved from that beginning.

I have chosen to present these selections with short translations accompanied by lengthy notes, and it is possible that some readers may make a charge of overinterpretation. The only answer to this is that *ko-uta* are by nature generally ambiguous, and it is this fact which gives them their interest. Unfortunately, a translation cannot capture the many layers of meaning contained in a single song. The notes attempt to remedy this fault by showing some of the possibilities contained in the original.

〈小唄〉

Since a great deal of *ko-uta*'s interest lies in highly involuted word play—a characteristic of much Edo-period literature—some explanation of the Japanese words is necessary. It is probably true that most Japanese who learn *ko-uta* today do not bother to analyze each song in the detailed way they are presented here. My teacher and the geisha I knew were often unable to explain the exact meaning of phrases that had been broken down, although the overall meaning or perhaps "feeling" of the song was clear to them. This is because the images run together and all tend to reinforce a particular mood which can be absorbed by a Japanese listener without phrase-by-phrase analysis.

While *ko-uta* have much in common with other genres of Japanese poetry and literature translated for Western readers, they still retain their own unique interest which I hope this small sampling manages to convey.

The calligraphy for the *ko-uta,* which is read from right to left and which appears here in the block form used in the Kasuga-school texts, was done by the master calligrapher Kaieda Shumpo (Miyaji Harumi) who has contributed to many major exhibitions in Japan and received the coveted Mainichi prize for brush work. The sample transcription of *Tomete mo Kaeru* was done by Judith Ann Herd, who also pointed out many aspects of the musical structure. This transcription is based on a tape recording and differs in some respects from the accompanying *shamisen* notation (p. 102), which was prepared from my own study materials. Susette Naylor did the sketch of the back view of the geisha on page 19. Black-and-white sketches were prepared for this volume by Hide Doki.

I am most grateful to my *ko-uta* teacher, Kasuga Nobu-
yuki, for her many hours spent in training my voice, and
the geisha of Pontocho, Kyoto, for showing me the true
spirit of the *ko-uta*. Also to Prof. Hiroshi Sakamoto of
Stanford University for his help with inscrutable gram-
mar. Finally, I am deeply indebted to Hasui Kiyo, ex-
geisha and presently mistress of the Maruki Inn, for her
perceptive interpretation when I was at a loss as to the
meaning of a song. This book is dedicated to her.

—LIZA CRIHFIELD

へ小唄∨

**18**

The characters on the fan read "Ichigiku,"
the name the author assumed as a geisha.

# THE KO-UTA

# 1   First Day of Spring

The spring wind whispers
Bring in fortune!
Fragrant plums breathe
Drive out devils!
Is it rain?
Is it snow?
I don't care—
We'll go on this evening
    and tomorrow too,
Drinking ginger saké.

*Haru kaze ga*
*Soyo soyo to*
*Fuku wa uchi e to*
*Kono yado e*
*Oni wa soto e to*
*Ume ga ka soyuru*
*Oya! Ame ka yuki ka*
*Mama yo mama yo*
*Kon'ya mo ashita mo*
*Itsuzuke ni*
*Shōgazake*

〈小
唄
〉

**20**

春風がそよ〳〵と福は内へ
とこの宿へ鬼は外へと梅が
香添ゆるおや雨か雪か盃
よく〳〵今宵もあ〳〵なも居
続けに生姜酒

This song is in the nature of a ditty describing some of the things associated with the festival of Setsubun (lit., "dividing the seasons") which marks the first day of spring in the lunar calendar. On this day one tosses beans from the veranda while exclaiming, "Devils out, Fortune in!" The plum trees are in bloom, and the drink of the day is a mildly alcoholic, milky type of saké with grated ginger in it. In this season the clouds may be producing either snow or rain, or perhaps both—it is the juncture between the seasons.

There is a classic case of a pivot word in *fuku* which may mean either "to blow" or "fortune," and, as it completes the first phrase, at the same time it puts us right into the second. The interjection "Is it rain? Is it snow?" is spoken within the context of the song, giving a humorous effect.

〈小唄〉

## 2  A Single Plum Blossom

A single plum blossom, then another
Opening one by one,
And the first plaintive notes
    of the bush warbler's song
Harbingers of the coming spring.
To tell the truth,
They only make me long
        to see you again. . . .


*Ume ichirin*

*Ichirin zutsu ni*

*Uguisu no*

*Utai some soro*

*Haru no keshiki mo*

*Totonou mama ni*

*Jitsu wa aitaku*

*Natta no sa*

There are a few *ko-uta* "good for any season," but most have a definite seasonal orientation. This is a spring song, and it mentions the traditional plum blossoms and *uguisu* ("bush warbler") motif that means "spring" to the Japanese just the way the first robin does to Westerners.

Although the first part of the song is sung "seriously," the last phrase, which appears wistful in writing, is given a twist of the voice which makes it very coquettish. The musical part was composed by Kasuga Toyo, a renowned teacher of *ko-uta*, for a poem of one of her friends. There is a section reminiscent of the musical style called *itchū-bushi*, which delights connoisseurs of the *shamisen*.

〈小唄〉

梅一輪一輪ずつに鶯（うぐいす）のう

たい初め候（そろ）春（はる）の景色（けしき）もと、

のうまに実（じつ）は違（ちが）いたく

なったのさ

## 3  Two Fans

Two fans overlapping,
An auspicious sign.
Like lovers embracing,
Two oak leaves.

A chrysanthemum's
Beauty is immortal but
For me,
Give me the color and
Fragrance of the plum.


*Kasane-ōgi wa*

*Yoi tsujiura yo*

*Futari shippori*

*Dakigashiwa*

*Kiku no hana nara*

*Itsu made mo*

*Ikete nagamete*

*Iru kokoro*

*Iro mo ka mo aru*

*Ume no hana*

重ね扇はよい辻占よ二人し
「ぽり抱きがしは菊の花な
らいつまでも活けて眺めて
いろころ色も香もある梅
の色

*Kasane-ōgi,* or "overlapping fans," with oak leaves is the family crest of a certain school of Kabuki actors. This whole song is an elaborate construction of double meanings which refer to two well-known Kabuki actors having this crest. It is most appreciated by the true *ko-uta* enthusiast who is naturally also well versed in the theater world. *Kiku,* or chrysanthemum, refers to the popular actor Kikugoro, with the meaning that "a performance by Kikugoro is not to be sneered at." The plum refers to Baiko, another actor, and it is obvious who this author is more partial to.

〈
小
唄
〉

**28**

# Evening Rain

Rain tonight it seems.
Drifting out of the clouds,
Even the moon is umbrellaed.
Resigned to a drenching,
The two of us
Moored together.
The rendezvous tree.

*Koyoi wa ame ka*

*Tsuki sae mo*

*Kasa kite izuru*

*Oboroyo ni*

*Nururu kakugo no*

*Fune no uchi*

*Sui ni moyaishi*

*Shubi no matsu*

During the latter part of the Tokugawa period (18th and early 19th centuries), the various pleasure quarters of the city of Edo were connected by a network of waterways built off the large rivers. The largest of the boats which plied those waters were big enough to hold drinking parties for more than ten persons, and smaller boats were used as ferries. At the approach of foul weather, the little boats would gather under one of the bridges for cover, and there are stories of rowdy scenes because of the close moorings. Someone would jostle another boat or peep behind the reed blinds into an intimate scene. The roofed boats, called *yakatabune,* had a connotation similar to that of the present-day "love motels," and the young men who piloted them had a reputation as a racy bunch.

The "rendezvous tree"in this song was a certain pine tree on the west bank of the Sumida River that was used as a landmark by those who were bound for the large brothel district called Yoshiwara. A couple wishing an hour or so of privacy could take one of the small boats and moor it by this tree where it would not arouse attention. The subjects of this song may be a geisha and her lover or perhaps one of the pilots of the boats.

In Japanese, the word *kasa* ("umbrella") written with a different Chinese character refers to the halo that sometimes floats around the moon at a change of weather. Phonetically, in this case, both meanings are implied and the word connects the rain, moon, wetness, and people, in a gradual shift from the description of nature to the erotic scene. The word *nururu,* "to be drenched," is also a pivot word with sexual connotations that connects the impending rain to the lovers' tryst in the boat.

The last phrase, *shubi no matsu,* while being the name of a particular tree, is homophonic with a phrase meaning "[I] wait for the consummation[of our love]." The erotic overtones of this song are so subtle as to be almost missed by a surface reading, but this is exactly what gives it *iroke.*

今宵は雨か月さえも暈

きえ出る朧夜に濡るゝ覚

惚の船の内粋にもやいし首

尾の松

## 5 Waiting Anxiously

Waiting anxiously for you,
Unable to sleep, but
    falling into a doze—
Are those words of love
Floating to my pillow,
Or is this too a dream. . . .
My eyes open and here is my
    tear-drenched sleeve.
Perhaps it was a sudden rain.


*Machiwabite*

*Neru to mo nashi ni*

*Madoromishi*

*Makura ni kayou*

*Kanegoto mo*

*Yume ka utsutsu ka*

*Utsutsu ka yume ka*

*Samete namida no*

*Sode tamoto*

*Are, murasame ga*

*Furu wai na*

待ちわびて寝るともなしに

まどろみし枕に通うかねご

とも夢か現かうつか夢か

覚めて涙の袖袂あれ村雨

が降るわいな

This song illustrates a common theme of *ko-uta*, namely that of the often blurry distinction between dreaming and reality, and the previously mentioned perception of nature through one's own emotional state. *Ko-uta* definitely come out of the Floating World genre of Japanese art and literature in which the Heian-period notion of the "impermanence of all things" in the Buddhist sense underwent a subtle change to the idea of the "transience of pleasure" in the Genroku period.

The word *murasame*, or "sudden rain," in the last stanza refers to unpredictable showers that start and stop, and carries a connotation of fickleness.

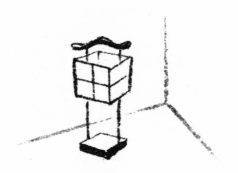

〈小唄〉

## 6  I'm Leaving

Please stay, I begged.
"I'm leaving."
I plead.
"I'm leaving."
*Hyoko hyoko* croaks the frog
As I leap through the
      back paddy fields
Disgraced, jilted,
In the falling rain.


*Tomete mo kaeru*

*Nadamete mo*

*Kaeru kaeru no*

*Mi hyoko hyoko*

*Tonda fushubi no*

*Ura tambo*

*Furare tsuide no, ē*

*Yoru no ame*

This song was composed around 1898 by a famous novelist named Ozaki Kōyō who was one of the founders of a literary movement described as "Neo-classicism." The goals of this group (called the Ken'yūsha, or "Friends of the Inkstone") were to recapture the preciosity of style and manner characteristic of earlier Tokugawa-period writers such as Saikaku. Ozaki Kōyō was a Tokyo roué who often frequented the pleasure quarters of that city. Stories of geisha, courtesans, and erotic encounters figure large as the subjects of his group's novels.

The setting of this song is Yoshiwara, where a guest is left by a woman. The man ends up walking home through the rice fields that extended behind Yoshiwara to the main part of town. To add insult to injury, or perhaps to intensify this feeling, it is raining in the bargain. The word *furare*, "to be spurned," also means "to be rained on."

There is a pun on the word *kaeru* which either means "frog," or "to leave [for home]" depending on the Chinese character. Different printed versions use one or the other or both, but when the song is heard, inevitably both images are evoked. The *hyoko hyoko* onomatopoeia describes a jumping frog, and the disgruntled customer seems to be saying, "All she says is *kaeru* [I'm leaving], she's just like a frog [*kaeru*], hopping away." The image of the back paddy fields and rain also strengthens the mental association with frogs.

へ
小
唄
∨

36 The score for *Tomete mo Kaeru* is provided in the Appendixes in both traditional *shamisen* and Western forms.

とめてもかえるなだめても
かえる〳〵のこゑひよこ〳〵と
んだ不首尾の裏田圃ふら
れつでのえ、夜の雨

## 7 Just Down the Road

I don't care a whit
What cherry tree blossoms
Just down the road.
I will stick with this tree
Petals scatter or stay—
My chosen man.

*Kono saki ni*

*Donna sakura ga*

*Sakō to mama yo*

*Watasha kono ki de*

*Kurō suru*

*Chiru mo chiranu mo*

*Nushi no mune*

The nice thing about *ko-uta* is that everyone seems to pick one or two to consider "his or her song." This one is a particular favorite of a middle-aged geisha I know who has been with her "chosen man" for close to twenty-five years now.

この先にどんな桜が咲こう
と、よわたしゃこの木で
苦労する　散るも　散らぬも
主の胸

## 8   In the Right Now of Now

In the right now of now,
Such things you say!
Two butterflies tied
By impossible dreams.
Yet we flutter along to
The end of the end.


*Ima no ima*

*Itta hito koto wa*

*Nikurashii*

*Adagoto na*

*Yume ni musubishi*

*Tsugai no chōchō*

*Sue no sue made*

*Futarizure*

*Ja wai na*

〈小唄〉

**40**

今のいま言った一言はにく
らしい仇言な夢に結びし
つがいの蝶〳〵末の末まで
二人連じゃわいな

This *ko-uta* is taken from the classical *gidayū* piece, *Chō no Michiyuki,* in which two lovers who cannot be united in life commit suicide and are changed into a pair of butterflies.

This song is sung from the woman's point of view, it seems. Her lover tells her he wants them to be together forever, and though that's unrealistic, she loves to hear him say so. Even if it's just a dream, she can imagine them as butterflies together till the end of time.

## 9 White Fans

White fans opened full
To the end of time
Our firm pledge
A silver node sparkling
Our vow holding us
     forever.
In the shade, pine boughs
Luxuriate in deep green.
The garden pool is clear
     as crystal,
Not a wave or breeze to
Ruffle its smooth surface.
Ah, what an enviable state!

This is a song for auspicious gatherings, especially weddings. Musically, it is rather stately (to the extent that a *ko-uta* can be) and it consists of a listing of what are considered favorable omens. It also shows the diversity of the *ko-uta* repertoire in which one may find a song for every feeling, for every occasion.

Hakusen no
Sue hirogari no
Sue kakete
Kataki chigiri no
Gin kaname
Kagayaku kage ni
Matsu ga e no
Ha-iro mo masaru
Fukamidori
Tachiyoru niwa no
Ike sumite
Nami kaze tatanu
Mizu no omo
Urayamashii de wa
Nai kai na

〈小唄〉
44

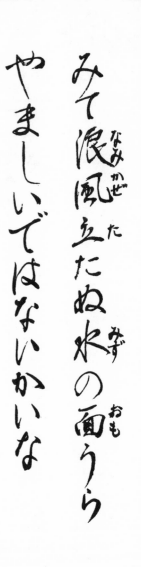

みて浪風立たぬ水の面うら
やましいではないかいな

白扇の末広がりの末かけ

て開き契りの銀安輝く影

に松が枝の葉色もまさる深

みどり立ち寄る庭の池澄

## After the Rain

The summer shower over
In the cool afternoon
A snowy egret stands
On one leg.

Preening on the bank
Its wind-ruffled wings.
In the back of the bay
From the tangled disarray
Of reeds, a woman's screams,
But behind this blind protest
It seems there is consent.

The boat in the bay
Dips and rises in turn
As gentle, then strong
Waves strike the stern.

This song is drawn from the Kabuki and classical dance repertoire for part of the story of Kozaru Shichinosuke. It depicts the famous rape scene which takes place in a small boat like the one described in *Ko Yoi wa Ame*.

It starts out in typical *ko-uta* fashion describing a scene from nature, then gradually the words take on double meanings, leading the listener into the details of the rape. It is possible both to read the entire song "straight" without any sexual imagery, on the one hand, and also to see innuendo in every phrase on the other. While the overlapping of images is complicated, it is the fact that an erotic scene can be subtly evoked with natural imagery, symbolism, and word play that makes this song interesting.

We may see examples of evocative ambiguity in the first few lines, where a sudden summer shower may be a symbol of a passionate encounter. The snowy egret, then, is implicitly compared to a fair-complexioned woman, and this image is strengthened by the bird preening its feathers the way a woman smooths her hair after making love.

From this point we have a flashback and the images become more explicit. The "disarray" may be of the reeds, or the woman's attire, and either may be bending in protest. Is it a woman's screams, or the waving reeds? At the end, we may take the meaning of a small boat bobbing in the back of the bay, or a boat poled from the stern, with sexual symbolism. High and low waves are called "male waves and female waves"; their rising and falling clearly suggests what is going on inside the boat.

Yūdachi no
Sugite suzushi ya
Shirasagi no
Kata-ashi agete
Kishi chikaku
Kaze no mae naru
Hazukuroi
Midare midareshi
Yoshi-ashi no
Iya ja iya ja wa
Ura no ura
Ura kogu fune no
Yuregokochi
Menami to onami ga
Uchiagete wa
Mata uchiorosu

ねのゆれごちみなみと男
なみがうちあげてはまたう
ちおろす

夕立ちのすぎて涼しや白

鷺の片足あげて岸近く風

のまえなる羽づくろいみだれ

みだれしよしのいやじゃく

はうらのうらうら漕ぐふ

## Sound of Insects

The insects have suddenly
    ceased chirping—
He's come!
Passing through the garden
    and opening the wicket gate—
It was only a falling paulownia leaf,
Hateful
Autumn sky with a
    crestfallen moon
Hiding behind the clouds.

*Mushi no ne o*

*Tomete ureshiki*

*Niwazutai*

*Akuru shiorido*

*Kiri hitoha, e*

*Nikurashii*

*Aki no sora*

*Tsuki wa shombori*

*Kumogakure*

〈小唄〉

**50**

虫の音をとめて嬉しき

庭づたいあくる柴折戸桐

一葉えく憐らしい秋の空月

はしよんぼり雲がくれ

This song may be taken as a prime example of how, in poetic Japanese sensibilities, natural phenomena and human feelings merge together. One waits with straining ears for a lover to come, then jumps up as the insects suddenly become quiet. Following then is the keen disappointment accompanying the realization that it was only the falling of a leaf that caused the change. Nature is then seen through bitter and disappointed eyes.

The original contains an ambiguity which may either be translated as "I'm so happy he is staying here tonight," or, as I have done, "[The insects] have suddenly ceased chirping." In view of the remainder of the song, the second interpretation seems to fit better.

In contrast to a purely personal descriptive style, Japanese poetry has a tendency to use certain "loaded" phrases that carry overtones of meaning familiar to readers who are acquainted with the literature. In this song, the "one paulownia leaf" (*kiri hitoha*) is an example. It is not an accident that it is the leaf of the *kiri* tree rather than some other leaf. A paulownia leaf falls swiftly without fluttering, symbolizing how quickly things may change—specifically, how suddenly autumn may arrive.

Phonetically, *kiri* also means "to sever," especially "to sever a relationship." Thus, the falling paulownia leaf carries a connotation of loneliness with the possibility that the awaited lover has been untrue.

Both the cries of insects and the paulownia are "season-marking" words, and this is clearly an autumn song.

〈小唄〉

## The Seven Autumn Grasses

Among the insects chirping
In the seven autumn grasses
Is the silent firefly, burning
With love
I pine for you
Even as the cries of the pine cricket
Taper off into the night.

The character for love
Is so very very important.


*Aki no nanakusa*

*Mushi no ne ni*

*Nakanu hotaru ga*

*Mi o kogasu*

*Kimi o matsumushi*

*Naku ne ni hosoru*

*"Koi" to iu ji wa*

*Taisetsu na*

秋の七草虫の音に鳴かぬ

蛍が身をこがす君をまつむし

鳴く音に細る恋と言う字

は大切な

There are insects that chirp and shrill and make a great to-do, and then there is the firefly which is silent but emits flashes of light. The various characters of the insects are implicitly compared to ways of demonstrating love— i.e., there are lovers who express themselves with eloquent words and fancy phrases, and there are those who are silent but whose love shines through. In either case, love is to be cherished.

The "seven autumn grasses" is a set concept for fall scenes, and is also a popular decorative motif in the graphic arts. The seven are: *hagi* (bush clover, lespedeza), *obana* (pampas grass), *kuzu* (arrowroot), *nadeshiko* (wild pink), *ominaeshi* (*Patrinia scabiosaefolia*), *fujibakama* (agueweed), and *kikyō* (Chinese bellflower).

**13**    ## Sprinkling the Garden

When I sprinkle the garden
Dewdrops sparkle on the grass.
The more I listen to the pathetic
    crying of insects
Burning with love
The more wretched I feel—
Who can be the cause of
    this pain?


*Uchimizu no*

*Shitataru kusa ni*

*Hikaru tsuyu*

*Koi ni kogarete*

*Naku mushi no*

*Koe o aware to*

*Kiku hodo no*

*Sabishii waga mi ni*

*Dare ga shita*

〈小唄〉

**56**

打水のしたゝる草に光る
露恋よこがれて鳴く虫の
声をあわれと聞くほどの寂
しい我が身に誰がした

As many of the *ko-uta* in this brief selection have illustrated, a person's innermost feelings become inextricably intertwined with the perception of nature. The phrase "burning with love" (*koi ni kogarete*) acts as a pivot between the insects and the author. In Japan, it is customary to sprinkle water on the garden before a guest is expected to arrive. One gets the sense in this *ko-uta* that preparations are being made for a guest who will never come. Also, when the crying of insects is mentioned (see also *Mushi no Ne*, no. 11, and *Aki no Nanakusa*, no. 12), it usually signifies loneliness, and may thus lend the song an autumn aura.

〈小唄〉

## Hoodwinked

To carouse
Is to be hoodwinked.

Yet even knowing so,
You're so skillful at it—
I'm helpless.

Water birds screeching and the
Taste of saké in the night.

*Damasarete*

*Iru no ga asobi*

*Namanaka ni*

*Damasu omae no*

*Te no umasa*

*Kuina kiku yo no*

*Sake no aji*

だまされているのがあそ

びなまなかにだますお前

の手のうまさ水鶏聞く夜

の酒の味

The subject of these songs usually remains unstated, so the songs can be seen from either a man's or a woman's perspective. This one, however, seems to be the lament of a customer in the geisha world who prefers to tolerate his favorite's philanderings rather than give her up. We can imagine her leaving the room—"just for a moment," she says—and him pouring himself a cup of saké while he waits for her return. The water bird *kuina* has a rather unpleasant voice which no doubt reflects the man's mood perfectly. *Kuina* written phonetically also denotes a kind of sullen, repressed feeling of grievance.

**First Snow**

Snowed in by the first falling flakes,
Between us a warm box of coals
    and the sound
    of a softly plucked *shamisen*.
My love and I, our heads together—
Is unreality the floating world, or the
    floating world the truth—
Heart to heart,
I cannot tell.

*Hatsuyuki ni*

*Furikomerarete*

*Mukōjima*

*Futari ga naka ni*

*Okigotatsu*

*Sasa no kigen no*

*Tsumebiki wa*

*Suita dōshi no*

*Sashimukai*

*Uso ga ukiyo ka*

*Ukiyo ga jitsu ka*

*Makoto kurabe no*

*Mune to mune*

初雪に降込められて向島
二人が中に置炬燵さへの機
嫌の尻弾はぬいた同志の差
何い噓が浮世か溚きが実か
誠くらべの胸と胸

The original of this song contains the word *Mukōjima* which is the name of a famous geisha district in Tokyo. To get there, one had to cross the Sumida River by boat, and this song describes the situation in which, because of the first snow of the season, it was difficult to return home. Thus, having a good excuse for staying, the customer happily nestles into the warm atmosphere with a favorite geisha. The softly plucked *shamisen* is being played with the fingernail instead of the usual large plectrum, and this also gives a note of added intimacy.

〈小唄〉

**64**

## 16  The Snowman

The snowman—
His charcoal eyes and nose
Melting, dribbling
    down his front,
Giving him a sooty black
    garment.

One of the shortest songs in the *ko-uta* repertoire, *Yuki no Daruma* nevertheless offers several possible levels of interpretation. On the surface, it is a *haiku*-like description of the children's winter playmate, who is melting with the onset of spring. At another level, it is a subtle jibe at Buddhist priests who sneak into brothels for a night of carousing.

The *sumigoromo*, or "sooty garment," is a commonly used designation for the bonze's black robes. A round face with a lump of a nose like a snowman's may refer to the ugly priest who is supposed to be pure but melts immediately at the sight of a woman. Alternatively, it may refer to even a dumpy courtesan who still has the power to "melt" the woman-hungry cleric.

Poking fun at Buddhist priests in the pleasure quarters has been material for satire throughout Japanese history.

*Yuki no daruma ni*
*Tadon no me hana*
*Tokete nagaruru*
*Sumigoromo*

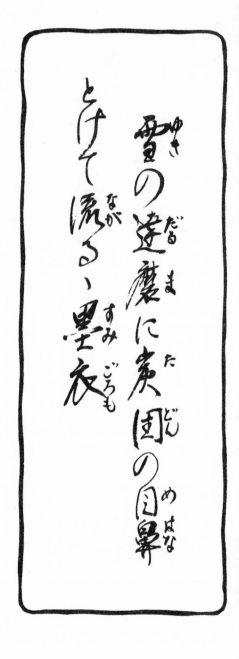

## The Charm of Tatsumi

The geisha of Tatsumi goes walking,
Bare white feet in black
  lacquered clogs.
In her *haori* jacket, she's
  the pride of Great Edo.
Ah, the Hachiman bell
  is ringing.


*Tatsumya yoi toko*
*Suashi ga aruku*
*Haori ya O-Edo no*
*Hokorimono*
*Hachiman-gane ga*
*Naru wai na*

巽（たつみ）やよいとこ素足（すあし）があるく

羽織（はおり）やお江戸（えど）のほこりもの

八幡鐘（はちまんがね）が鳴（な）るわいな

As in many ko-uta, the place name Tatsumi evokes images of the geisha world. In the Tokugawa period, Tatsumi, close to the castle, was an area where the geisha were renowned for their skill in the arts. Of all the geisha, they alone were permitted to wear haori jackets over their kimono, and this was seen as a mark of their pride. Another such affectation was the fact that they never wore tabi socks, but went barefooted in geta (sandals) even in the dead of winter. The Hachiman shrine mentioned is where people from that section of town went to pray.

The word hokori, which I have translated as "pride," was, according to some interpretations, originally the hokori which means "dust," and a reference to the fact that a haori is worn to keep the dust off one's kimono. Presently, it is the former meaning which is most accepted.

The shamisen accompaniment to this song contains a section drawn from the ji-uta style, known as "Yuki" (Snow). It is used as a musical motif in Kabuki drama or other compositions when the text mentions a winter scene. Here, it occurs after the phrase "walking barefooted" (suashi ga aruku), and though snow is not mentioned directly in the text, a listener familiar with the shamisen motifs would recognize the hint and picture the proud geisha in the winter.

## Cold-Water Tea

Cold water can't brew
A fragrant tea,
Nor does our fate
Decree that we
　　　may be one.
Still, let them think
　　　what they will—
I will never
Leave your side.


Mizu no debana to

Futari no naka wa

Sekare awarenu

Mi no inga

Tatoe donata no

Iken demo

Omoi omoikiru ki wa

Sara ni nai

〈小唄〉

**70**

水の出花と二人の仲は

せかれあわれぬ身の因果

たとえどなたの意見でも

思い切る気は更にない

This song is often considered the most representative of the *ko-uta* repertoire and usually is the first piece a new student learns. For all its popularity, the meaning is unusually obscure, and while the general impression of the song is understandable, even *ko-uta* enthusiasts have trouble with the phrase *mizu no debana*.

One possible meaning is "flowers floating down a stream," but there is another, more involved, possible meaning. We may see *debana* as originally the word for "fragrance of the first brew of tea." The term was later sometimes used as an alternate word for tea itself, especially in the pleasure quarters.

There was an aversion to using the word tea (*cha*) because of a complicated etymology attributing bad luck to the word *cha*. To say *ocha o hiku*, or "to grind tea," referred to women who had no customers and were put to this task to keep them busy—a state of affairs not conducive to prosperous business in Yoshiwara. Hoping to avoid this situation, people superstitiously refrained from even mentioning the word *cha*, and instead used alternate terms like *debana*.

In any case, fragrant tea cannot be made with *mizu* (cold water), thus the gist of these lines seems to be a comparison of this kind of impossibility with an impossible love.

A related nuance is a custom of marking the end of an affair by the exchange of cups of water instead of saké. Water has connotations of instability and separation in Japanese. We say "gone with the wind" in English; the Japanese express the same sentiment with water. Here

〜
小
唄
〜
**72**

the meaning of flowers floating down a stream (implying floating apart) also conveys this sense of hopeless love.

This song most likely describes a love affair between a geisha or courtesan and a man who perhaps doesn't have the money to buy his sweetheart out of bondage. They cannot marry, and are causing a scandal by their infatuation, but the singer refuses to be shaken in her (it seems to me to be sung from the woman's point of view) passionate attachment.

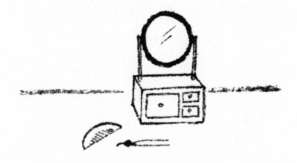

Lovers' Quarrel

There are times I just get
    so peeved,
I pour a bowlful of saké—
Then hesitate
    before downing it.
"Well, if you're not going to
    drink it,
Give it to me. . . ."
Back and forth, we get
    roaring drunk.
This is how we resolve
A lovers' quarrel.

*Hara no tatsu tokya*

*Chawan de sake o*

*Nomedo nomenu*

*Nomenu sake nara*

*Sukete mo yaro ga*

*Iya nara suikyō na*

*Okashanse*

*Otto! Sokora ga*

*Kuzetsu no*

*Tane to naru*

〈小
唄
〉

**74**

腹の立つときや茶碗び酒
を飲めど飲めぬ飲めぬ酒な
らすけてもやうがいやなら
酔狂なおかしゃんせおと
そくらが口舌の種となる

One of the earthier *ko-uta*, this one describes a conjugal spat and its resolution. The title literally translates as "when my stomach stands up"—a common colloquial phrase in Japanese that gives interesting imagery to the state of being angry.

An alternate interpretation may be that this is a geisha who has just had a falling out with her patron and has retired to her room in a huff. Pouring a huge cup of saké, she sits and stews. There is another man in the background who has had his eye on her for some time and sees this as a chance to press his case. Going in, he offers to help her drink (drinking alone has a sharp connotation of loneliness), and she forgets her previous quarrel in the discovery of a new love.

〈小唄〉

**76**

**20**

## Longing

Longing, longing
To be together
I fret my days away.
Ever so once in a while
We steal a night together,
    and part
Longing, longing.

Parting is merely longing,
    never farewell—
The temple bell sounding
    at dawn.

*Sekare sekarete*
*Kuyo kuyo kurasu e*
*Tama ni au yo wa*
*Sekarete wa ai*
*Ōte wa sekare*
*Wakare to mo nai*
*Ake no kane*

せかれ〳〵てよく〳〵暮すえ

たまにあう夜はせかられては

逢い逢うてはせかれ別れと

もない明の鐘

Many geisha feel that this is "their song." Because of the nature of the work a geisha does, she is not free to be with her man as much as she would like—perhaps he is married, perhaps she is busy with other engagements. So if a burning love affair occurs in a geisha's life, the result is most likely to be feelings that will be expressed by this song.

The bell which sounds at dawn by striking six times means that the lovers will have to separate. A piece from the classical *naga-uta* repertoire has the title *Ake no Kane* (Dawn's Bell) and the story compares a woman's grief to the melancholy reverberation of the bell at dawn.

## 21 Journeying Lovestruck

On my lovestruck journey
Nothing I fear,
Striding tonight
    on these lonely dark roads,
Knowing I'm going to see her again.
(I'll bet she's not even
    thinking of me. . . .)
Still, I'll cross over mountains for her.
If there were some way
To see her each night—
What bliss!
Is there no way?
Impassioned impasse.

This is a song of unrequited love, but we are struck by the determination of the hero. He knows that his efforts may very well be in vain, but he cannot give up at this point. Because of the image of traveling across mountains, it is possible that this song is about a farmer's lad who visits the object of his affections in a neighboring village. However, the word for "climbing [a mountain]" (*noboritsumeru*) also means "to visit a house in the pleasure quarters often," so it is equally conceivable that it is the lament of a customer in love with a courtesan.

Horete kayou ni
Nani kowakarō
Koyoi mo aō to
Yami no yomichi o
Tada hitori
Sakya sahodo ni mo
Omoyasenu no ni
Kocha noboritsume, ē
Yama o koete
Ai ni yuku
Dō shita en de
Ka no hito ni
Maiban ōtara
Ureshikaro
Dō surya
Sowareru en ja yara
Jirettai yo!

ゆくどうした縁で彼の人に毎晩逢うたら嬉しいかろどうすりゃ添われる縁じゃやらじれったいよ

惚（ほ）れて通（かよ）うた何（なに）うわか

ろう 今宵（こよい）も逢（あ）おうと暗（やみ）の

夜路（よみち）を唯（ただ）一人（ひとり）先（さき）やさほどた

も思（おも）やせぬのにこちゃ登（のぼ）り

つめて山（やま）を越（こ）えて逢（あ）いに

## 22 Closing Time Is Midnight

Closing time is midnight—
So why do I now hear
The wooden clappers
Strike out four times?

In Yoshiwara, even the
Wooden rhythm sticks
are liars.


*Hike wa kokonotsu*
*Naze sore o yotsu*
*To iuta ka*
*Yoshiwara wa*
*Hyōshigi made mo*
*Uso o tsuku*

〈小唄〉

引けは九つなぜそれを四つと言うたか　吉原は拍子木までもうそをつく

This song is a section lifted directly from the *naga-uta* classical music piece *Miyako Fūryū* (Scenes from the Capital). Yoshiwara was the largest of the *yūkaku* (walled-in prostitute sections, or pleasure quarters) in Edo. Yoshiwara officially closed its main gate at ten o'clock at night, but a small door was left open (for those in the know) until midnight, *kokonotsu,* or "the ninth hour" in the old system of measuring time. At midnight then, the wooden clappers would sound out four times signaling "ten o'clock"—thus the accusation that, in Yoshiwara, besides the prostitutes (who were quite famous for their skill with untruths), even the wooden clappers were liars.

〈小唄〉

**86**

**23** Wine and Women

Wine and women
Balm for the soul,
This floating world *is*
Women and wine.
Just a taste, and now
Karma leads me to this fate.
Praise the lord, praise the lord!
To heaven or hell,
Women and wine.
You and me, babe
Till the end—
With a honey like you
With me in hell,
Emma and Jizō might forget
They ever renounced the world.
Oh, the demon drink!

なけれども お前の様な美しい女

子と地獄へゆくならば閻魔

さんでも地蔵さんでもまた〱

〱 鬼ころし

酒と女は気の薬さ　とかく
浮世は色と酒さ、ちょっぴり
つまんだ　悪縁因縁南まいだ
くく　地獄極楽へずっとりゅく
のも二人連　わしが敕目じゃ

*Sake to onna wa*

*Ki no kusuri sa*

*Tokaku ukiyo wa*

*Iro to sake, sa sa*

*Choppiri tsumanda*

*Akuen innen*

*Namaida namaida namaida*

*Jigoku gokuraku e*

*Zutto yuku no mo*

*Futarizure*

*Washi ga yokume ja*

*Nakeredomo*

*Omae no yō na*

*Utsukushii*

*Onago to*

*Jigoku e yuku naraba*

*Emma-san demo*

*Jizō-san demo*

*Mada mada mada mada mada*

*Onigoroshi*

〈
小
唄
〉

**90**

This song varies a bit from the usual *ko-uta* in its straight-forward bantering tone, and a rhythmic pattern that breaks out of the usual five-and-seven-syllable mode intensifies the humor. It was composed in the latter part of the Edo period by wandering minstrels who made their way from town to town entertaining people with their arts. The middle section is spoken rather than sung, and is something like a Japanese tongue-twister.

Emma is the king of the Buddhist hell, and Jizō is a Buddhist deity who is the patron saint of travelers. The last word, *onigoroshi*, literally means "demon killer," and was the name of a cheap type of alcohol which was the drink of these peripatetic minstrels, not able to afford good saké.

Marionette

Your heart
Flip-flops and changes
Like a marionette.
There's someone in the shadows
Pulling your strings.

*Karakuri no*
*Patto—kawarishi*
*Omae no kokoro*
*Kage de ito hiku*
*Hito ga aru*

*Karakuri* was a type of mechanical puppet device popular in the early part of this century. Here, the slighted lover accuses his (her) partner of fickle-heartedness by the comparison to the marionette.

からくりのぱこと変りし
お前の心かけで糸引く人
がある

## Snake Mountain

(PROLOGUE)

Up at the hermitage on Snake Mountain,
Lighting the bonfire for All Souls,
Suddenly—
The paper lantern bursts open and
*Hyū, doro doro*
Goblins and changelings creep out.

The ghost of poor Iwa-san
Holding her baby,
Slain by Iemon, left
Cradling a stone buddha
Hee, hee, hee . . .

〈小唄〉

**94**

So it goes
If you're cruel to a woman.
But—
Pamper her,
She puffs with conceit.
You don't suit her fancy,
Her rage can't be beat.
Reprove her, she cries,
And philander—before your eyes,
Two sprouting horns
Of jealousy arise.
But—
Just knock her off
And she'll haunt you
Sure enough.
A woman is a fearful thing—
Though we can't do without them,
Best take care, best
        take care—
A woman is a fearful thing
        indeed!

*Hebi yama no*
*Anshitsu de*
*Mukaibi takeba*
*Kadoguchi no*
*Chōchin no naka kara*
*Hyū, doro doro to*
*Bakete deta no wa*
*O-Iwa-san*
*Akago to itsuwari*
*Iemon ni*
*Ishi jizō dakasete*
*Hi hi hi . . .*

\*

*Kore mo onna ni*
*Jaken kara*
*Yasashiku sarereba*
*Tsukeagari*
*Ki ni iranakereba*
*Okoridashi*
*Kogoto o iwarerya*
*Jiki ni naki*
*Uwaki o sarereba*
*Tsuno o dasu*
*Sari tote koroseba*
*Bakete deru*
*Hontō ni onna wa*
*Kowai mono*
*To wa ie inakerya*
*Komaru deshō*
*Mina-san seizei*
*Goyōjin, hā hā*
*Kowaya no kowaya no*
*Korya korya korya*

〈小唄〉

**96**

蛇山の庵室でむかい火た

けば門口のちょうちんの中か

らヒュウドロ〜と化けて出たの

はお岩さん赤子といつわり

伊右衛門に石地蔵だかせてヒヒヒ……

*(to top of p. 99)*

化けて出る本当に女はこわいも
のとは言え居なけりゃこまる
でしょう皆さんせいぐ＼／御用
心＼／こわやの＼／＼／ユリヤく
＼

こうれも女（おな）にじゃけんからやさ

しくされゝばつけ上（あが）り気（き）に入（い）

らなければ怒（おこ）り出（だ）しふ言（こと）を

言われりや直（じき）に泣（な）き浮気（うき）をさ

れば角（つの）を出（だ）すさりとて殺（こう）せば

The prologue to this song sets the stage for the author's misogynist diatribe by mentioning a scene from the well-known collection of ghost stories, *Yotsuya Kaidan*. In the tale of Iwa-san and Iemon, Iemon murders his wife in order to take another bride, but he wants to take his child by Iwa-san along with him. As Iemon then hurries off after the foul deed, the baby in his arms, Iwa-san appears as a ghost and he finds the child he was carrying has turned into a small stone statue. The ghost of Iwa-san laughs eerily, having gotten her revenge.

The second section of this song is constructed in a rhythm of five- and eight-syllable lines (rather than five and seven), which gives it a "sing-song" effect, and it is punctuated with colloquial interjections.

〈小唄〉

**100**

*APPENDIXES*

## 1. Shamisen Notation for *Tomete mo Kaeru*

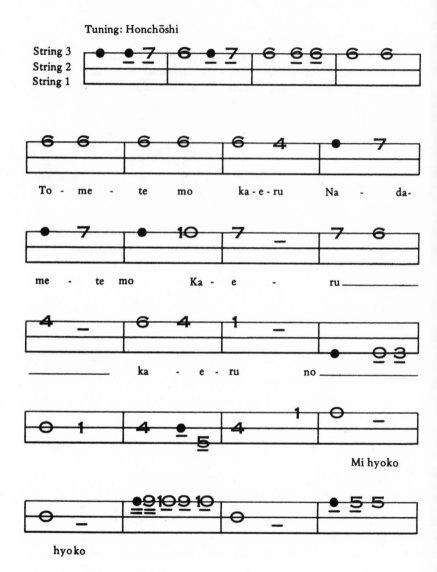

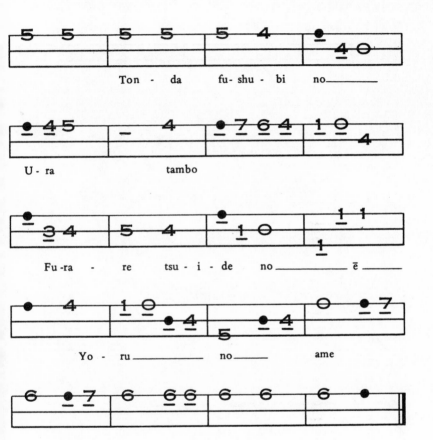

TUNING: *Honchōshi*, strings 1 and 3 tuned an octave apart;
string 2 tuned to the interval of a fourth from string 1.

## 2. Western Transcription of *Tomete mo Kaeru*

| | | |
|---|---|---|
| **I** | **∧** | **ᵕ** |
| Breath mark | Pitch unclear | Rhythmically weak note |

## THE TALE OF GENJI

*by Murasaki Shikibu, translated by Kencho Suematsu*
ISBN 0-8048-3256-0

This biographical novel centers around the amorous exploits of Prince Hikaru Genji, whose elegance and talent epitomized the values of Heian Japan, an era in which indigenous Japanese culture still held prominence over the Chinese culture that would come to dominate Japan.

## THE JOURNEY

*a Novel about Japan in the
Aftermath of the American Occupation
by Jiro Osaragi, translated by Ivan Morris*
ISBN 0-8048-3255-2

This touching allegorical novel about a man who is almost destroyed by his lust for money and the accumulation of wealth is a masterful depiction of the new moral reality facing post-war Japan.

## THE BUDDHA TREE

*by Fumio Niwa, translated by Kenneth Strong*
ISBN 0-8048-3254-4

The author's remarkable insight into human weaknesses, his sensitive sketches of the Japanese countryside, and his revelation of the materialism of the modern Buddhist church in Japan, make this a book of unusual distinction.

## KAPPA

*A Satire By The Author Of Rashomon
by Ryunosuke Akutagawa, translated by Geoffrey Bownas*
ISBN 0-8048-3251-X

A Swiftian satire of Japanese society thinly disguised as the fictitious Kappaland. Peopled with creatures rom Japanese folklore, Kappaland serves as a vehicle :or the humorous examination of the moral foibles of Japanese society in the early 20th century.

## THE COUNTERFEITER
## AND OTHER STORIES

*by Yasushi Inoue, translated by Leon Picon*
ISBN 0-8048-3252-8

These three short stories, "The Counterfeiter," "Obasute," and "The Full Moon," explore the roles of loneliness, compassion, beauty, and forgiveness in day-to-day life in Japan, all within the context of the Buddhist-influenced notion of inescapable predestination.

## ROMAJI DIARY AND SAD TOYS

*by Takuboku Ishikawa
translated by Sanford Goldstein and Seishi Shinoda*
ISBN 0-8048-3253-6

The novella *Romaji Diary* represents the first instance of a Japanese writer using romaji (roman script) to tell stories in a way that could not be told in kana or kanji. *Sad Toys* is a collection of 194 tanka, the traditional 31-syllable poems that are evocative of Japan's misty past and its tentative steps into the wider world.

## FIRES ON THE PLAIN

*by Shohei Ooka, translated by Ivan Morris*
ISBN: 0-8048-1379-5

Based on the author's experience as a prisoner captured by American forces during WWII, *Fires on the Plain* tells the story of the disintegration of Private Tamura, a Japanese soldier during the dark end days of the war. One by one, each of his ties to society is destroyed, until Tamura, a sensitive and intelligent man, becomes an outcast.

## THE IZU DANCER
## & OTHER STORIES

*by Yasunari Kawabata and Yasushi Inoue*
ISBN 0-8048-1141-5

Four stories from two of Japan's most beloved and acclaimed fiction writers. "The Izu Dancer" was the story that first introduced Kawabata's prodigious talent to the West. Stories by Inoue include, "The Counterfeiter," "Obasute," and "The Full Moon."